FAMILY TIME
TRAINING

Bible
Activities
and Object
Lessons
for Families
with
Children
of All Ages

Seeing is Believing

KIRK WEAVER

To Jim Weidmann, who introduced me to the priceless joy and peace that comes from providing intentional spiritual training in the home. To my family—Kelly, Madison, and McKinley—who have embraced Family Time as a core value in our life together. And, to our unborn grandchildren and great-grandchildren, may you learn, live, and teach Jesus as our personal Savior and eternal hope.

To Melvina Killion, who has provided encouragement, advice, and support to me and to Family Time Training from the beginning. She has a love for children and shares God's vision for building strong families. I count knowing Melvina as one of the greatest blessings of my life.

—*Kirk Weaver*

Table of Contents

Family Activities

Teaching Goal: When Christ is the foundation of our lives, we can stand firm.
Scripture: Matthew 7:24-27

Teaching Goal: Our value comes from God.
Scripture: Romans 5:8, John 3:16, Psalm 8:5-7

Teaching Goal: God, Jesus, and the Holy Spirit are one.
Scripture: Mark 1:10-11, Matthew 28:19

Teaching Goal: Jesus is our guide to get through the traps in life.
Scripture: Joshua 23:12-13

Teaching Goal: Believe in Jesus even when you can't see him.
Scripture: John 20:24-29

Teaching Goal: Fill our home with the fragrant aroma of Christ.
Scripture: 2 Corinthians 2:14-15, Deuteronomy 5:7-21, 2 Corinthians 12:20, 2 Corinthians 4:2, Galatians 5:20-23, Matthew 15:19

Teaching Goal: God wants us to learn about him in our home.
Scripture: Deuteronomy 6:5-9

Mission

The mission of Family Time Training is to reach future generations with the Good News of Christ by training parents to teach their children Christian principles, values, and beliefs in the home.

Vision Statement

Imagine a child who responds to the needs of others and is eager to give and share.

Imagine a child who has learned to say "no" to busyness. A child who will take time to slow down and who understands the necessity of Sabbath rest.

Imagine a child who has been trained to seek truth.

Imagine a child who lives accountable to an unseen but always present God.

Imagine a child whose best friend is Jesus.

Imagine a child who is more eager to learn about the teachings of Jesus than to watch television or play sports.

Imagine a child with an eternal perspective, a child who invests more time giving and serving than accumulating and being entertained.

Imagine hundreds and thousands, a whole generation, of children growing up to live and teach the example of Christ.

In Deuteronomy 6:7 God presents his plan for passing on a godly heritage to our children. At Family Time Training our vision is to see future generations living for Christ. First, parents are to be the primary spiritual teachers in the lives of children. Second, spiritual training is to take place 24 hours a day, seven days a week. Family Time Training is just a tool, but it is a tool God can use in your family to accomplish his vision.

Foreword

"I believe most parents who are Christian want to teach their children the faith, they just don't know how. The church is important support but primary spiritual teaching must happen in the home, otherwise, it's not going to happen."

—R.C. Sproul, theologian

Family Time is the "how to" tool parents can use to teach their children the faith at home. The organization Family Time Training equips parents with fun and exciting activities designed to teach children Christian principles, values, and beliefs.

Family Time Training was formed in response to a spiritual crisis that threatens to undermine the foundation of today's families. For generations, Christian parents have abdicated to the church their God-given role as the primary spiritual leaders for their children. The church is expected to build within the lives of children a strong spiritual foundation in just one or two hours per week. God designed spiritual training to take place 24 hours a day, seven days a week, with the parents providing primary leadership and the church providing important support. For the sake of our children we must return proactive spiritual training to the home.

Family Time Training works with churches, schools, and spiritually-based groups to teach parents how to provide home-based spiritual training. Training is provided through sermons, classes, and weekend seminars. Families receive direct support through a website (www.famtime.com), activity books, and quarterly mailings.

—Kirk Weaver

Introduction

Not long ago, my wife Kelly and I were talking with Madison on her bed in her room. She was upset with the kids at school. Some were picking on an unpopular student, playing a cruel game Madi chose not to play, and it left her separated from her girlfriends. With tears flowing down her face, Madi said, "I'm trying to be like the beans in Dad's story."

Madi was referring to a Family Time lesson. The activity is built around three pots of boiling water, with the water representing adversity. We drop a carrot into the first pot, an egg into the second, and coffee beans into the third. What choices will we make in response to the adversity we face in our lives? Do we get soft like the carrot the way Peter did when he denied Christ? Does the adversity make us hard like the egg and Pharaoh's heart? Or like the coffee beans, which can represent the example of Paul, do we influence and change the environment around us? Madi was applying a lesson that we'd taught more than four months earlier.

As a parent, you've had moments like this. You know what they're worth.

Family Time activities are simple, fun object lessons intended to teach children about life in God's world. This is a book of ideas for structured teaching times that will carry forward and open doors for informal learning moments. At first it may feel a little clumsy to create the structured time, to boil carrots and eggs and coffee beans. But the moments when your child actively chooses the godly path will fuel your love and your relationship like nothing else in the world.

"Here's the game," I told the four children, my son, daughter, and two neighborhood friends. They were standing at the bottom of the stairs, wide-eyed and eager for the Family Time activity. Standing at the top of the stairs, I said, "I represent Jesus in heaven. More than anything I want you up here with me, but, you can't use the stairs and you can't use the handrails."

They knew there was a trick, something to learn. But what? How would they get from the bottom of the stairs to the top without touching the stairs or the railing? My daughter ran to get a laundry basket, turned it upside down, stood on top and reached up only to find she was still more than fifteen steps from the top.

It was my son, Mac, the youngest of the four, who figured out the solution. "I got it! Dad, please come down and get me," his face beaming, because he had solved the riddle. I descended the stairs.

"Will you carry me to the top?" he asked. "Of course!" I responded. After carrying all four children piggyback style to the second floor, I said, "That's how you get to heaven. You can't do it on your own. Only through Jesus can you get there." A powerful lesson presented in the language of children that they still remember to this day.

Deuteronomy 6:5-9 says:
"Love the LORD your God with all your heart and with all your soul and with all your strength. These commandments that I give you today are to be upon your hearts. Impress them on your children."

How?
"Talk about them when you sit at home and when you walk along the road, when you lie down and when you get up. Tie them as symbols on your hands and bind them on your foreheads. Write them on the doorframes of your houses and on your gates."

How will we shape our children? What mark will we leave upon them? Is it possible that we can launch them into the world stronger, purer, more trusting of God than we were? Is it possible that we can reshape our families and our family interactions around the joy of loving God with all that is within us?

I believe it is possible. That's what this book is for.

The ABC's of Effective Family Times

A▶ Attention Span: The rule of thumb for attention span is one minute for each year of age. A three-year-old may have a three-minute attention span. Break up your Family Time into three-minute increments. With variety, you gain additional attention span. For example:

3 minutes	Sing or play your Family Time theme song
2 minutes	Pray
3 minutes	Tell the story
3 minutes	Demonstrate the object lesson
3 minutes	Let the child repeat the object lesson
3 minutes	Retell the story
2 minutes	Practice memorization
2 minutes	Close in prayer

21 minutes	Total Family Time

B▶ Be Prepared to Say "I Don't Know": Your children WILL ask you a question that you cannot answer. Promise to find the answer and get back to them within 24 hours. You can call a pastor or search the Internet for more information.

C▶ Call it Family Time: When your children grow up you want them to have fond, lasting memories of Family Time. When referring to your times of formal spiritual training, say "Family Time" often. In the same way your children will remember going to school and church or playing sports and music, they will remember times of spiritual training called "Family Time."

D▶ Drama Queens and Kings: Kids love to put on plays. Pick a Bible Story, assign the roles from Director to Diva—everyone gets in on the act. Don't forget to assign a videographer so you can watch it later.

E **Encourage Guessing:** Answering a question involves risk. Your child's answer may be right or wrong. Praise him when he guesses at an answer. If he gives the wrong answer say, "Great guess! The answer is..." and give him the correct information. This will keep him participating. If you say, "No, that's wrong," children may eventually stop talking.

F **Fixed or Flexible:** It's great and admirable to have Family Time the same night every week. However, it may not be practical for your family. Be willing to move the night if needed. The important thing is to have at least one Family Time each week.

G **Give it to God:** God commands parents and grandparents to be spiritual teachers with their children (Deuteronomy 6:7; Deuteronomy 4:9, Psalm 78:5). Trust that God will equip you to fulfill his plan. As you prepare, and before you begin your Family Time each week, pray and ask the Holy Spirit to lead you and clearly communicate the message to your children.

H **Hold the Distractions:** When sitting at the table, remove the centerpiece, pencils, paper...anything that can distract a child. A random paper clip left on a table can lead to a possession battle that will ruin the atmosphere for Family Time. Also, when using materials like balloons, string, etc., don't bring them out until you're ready to use them.

I **Involve Kids in the Preparations:** Whenever possible, especially as kids get a little older, involve kids in the lesson preparations. Preparation can be as much fun as doing the activity and certainly increases ownership. Kids will enjoy making an obstacle course, building a tent with sheets, or mixing a big batch of cornstarch.

J **Just Do It!:** Don't wait another day to get started!

K **Kitchen Table:** Start your Family Time at the kitchen table even if you are only going to be there for a few minutes. Chairs provide natural boundaries that will help children focus as you explain what will happen during the Family Time.

L Listen to the Holy Spirit: Be prepared to modify or change the discussion if the Spirit moves the conversation in a different direction.

M Make a Picture: Coloring a picture to reinforce a Bible Story can be an excellent teaching technique. While the family is coloring, great conversation about the lesson can take place.

N Not a Spectator Sport: Participate with your children in the game or activity. By participating, you show your kids that you value Family Time.

O Oh Boy! If you're feeling frustrated or if family members have a negative attitude—reschedule. Keep it positive.

P Play it Again, Sam: For younger children, put the lesson into a one sentence phrase like: "Noah had faith in God." Or, "Be content with what God sent." The same night at bedtime, remind children of the main point. The following morning ask them what they remember from Family Time the night before.

Q Quitting isn't an Option: Commit to once a week and do your best not to take a week off. Continue to do Family Time during the summer months. If you stop, your kids will sense a lack of commitment to Family Time on your part.

R Repetition isn't the Same as Redundant: Younger children learn best through repetition. In the same way they will watch a video over and over, they may want to repeat fun Family Time activities. Be prepared to repeat the activity, asking the children to explain what the different elements represent. Consider repeating with neighborhood children; your children will learn even more when they teach others.

S Simple Structure: Younger children benefit from a structured time together. Consider following the Family Time Format each week.

T **To Be or Not to Be Silly:** Model for your children that it's okay to be dramatic, silly, and have fun. Kids love it when their parents are playful.

U **Unique Locations:** Have a church service in a crawl space to represent the early church under persecution. Hold your Family Time outside at a neighborhood park. Repeat fun activities when visiting relatives on vacation. Tell the story of Zacchaeus while sitting in a tree house. Changing the setting of your Family Time can be fun.

V **Variety:** Using a video clip can be an excellent way to teach a lesson. However, using video clips three weeks in a row becomes predictable and is less effective. Mix up the format and tools you use in your weekly Family Time (coloring, video clips, a snack tied to the lesson, etc.).

W **Watch Out for Unrealistic Expectations:** Family Time is seldom a disappointment to children. However, parents may sometimes feel like the lesson did not go as well as they had hoped. Often this disappointment is directly related to the parent's expectations. Keep in mind that kids learn valuable things over time. You don't have to get something fantastic out of each Family Time. Be prepared to learn right along with your kids.

X **Xpect a Future:** One day your children will grow up and start families of their own. As your children raise your grandchildren they will be equipped with positive memories and effective tools to pass along the faith of their fathers.

Y **Y? Y? Y?** Questions are cool. Frederick Beuchner says, "If you want big answers then ask small questions." "What did you learn at Sunday School?" is a big question. "Who did you sit next to at Sunday School?" is a smaller question that can lead to more discussion.

Z **Zees ees Fun!** Remember the most important things you can do: take your time, engage your child, and have fun together. A silly accent never hurts either!

Family Time Format

The "Family Time Format" is a simple structure that families can use when leading a Family Time activity. You may want to tweak and modify the structure to meet the needs of your family.

Younger children benefit from using the same format from week to week. They may want to repeat the activity again and again. Remember, repetition is how young children learn. Be sure to call your time together "Family Time." When your kids are grown, you want them to look back and be able to identify times of formal spiritual training in the same way they can identify school, sports, and church.

Families of older children may want to make the lesson less formal. For example, you may not have a "Family Time Theme Song." Instead, you can invite your teens to share a favorite song. Ask them why they like the song. Is it the beat, the singer, the words?

Meet Weekly:
The goal is to lead a weekly Family Time in your home. Try to designate and reserve the same time each week, recognizing that on occasion you will need the flexibility to schedule around conflicts.

No Fuss Dinner:
Plan a simple dinner so that everyone in the family can participate. You don't want one parent spending a lot of time fixing the meal and another parent spending a lot of time cleaning up. Minimize dinner preparation and clean-up by using paper plates and paper cups. Just by looking at how the table is set, children will know it's Family Time night. You may want to use leftovers or order in dinner. Keep it simple.

Discuss the Previous Family Time:
During dinner talk about what the family did last week during Family Time. Challenge the children to try and remember the activity and message. Talk about the

highlights and use this time to reinforce the message and its potential application during the past week.

You'll be surprised to learn that children will remember back two weeks, three weeks, maybe more.

Family Time Theme Song:

Pick your own family "theme song." Since this is for your spiritual training time, consider songs that talk about faith, family, relationships, and love.

Play this song after dinner and just before the evening lesson and activity. Younger children like to create a dance or hand motions to go with the song. This song signals that Family Time is here while building excitement and anticipation.

SONG IDEAS:
"The Family Prayer Song (As For Me and My House)" by Maranatha
"Creed" by Rich Mullins

Prayer:

Open the Family Time with prayer. Children and parents can take turns. Teach the children to pray about a wide variety of topics, joys, and concerns.

Message:

Decide in advance and practice the activity you will use. Communicate clearly the main principle or value being taught through the lesson.

Object Lesson:

Each Family Time has an object lesson or activity that reinforces and helps children remember the main message.

Memorize:

Repeat the short, rhyming phrase included with the lesson. The rhyme is designed to help children remember the lesson.

Prayer:

Close the time together with a prayer. Tie the prayer to the lesson. Try different methods of prayer such as holding hands and praying, pray from oldest to youngest, or say "popcorn" prayers (one- or two-word prayers about a specific topic).

Plan Ahead for Next Week:

Many lessons require that you gather specific objects or purchase items from the store. Look ahead to next week's Family Time activity to make sure you have all the necessary ingredients.

Lesson 1:
BUILD YOUR HOUSE ON THE ROCK

 TEACHING GOAL: When Christ is the foundation of our lives, we can stand firm.

1. Play theme song
2. Pray
3. Lesson and discussion
4. Memorize: **On Christ the solid rock I stand; all other ground is sinking sand.**
5. Close in prayer

 SCRIPTURE: Matthew 7:24-27 "Therefore everyone who hears these words of mine and puts them into practice is like a wise man who built his house on the rock. The rain came down, the streams rose, and the winds blew and beat against that house; yet it did not fall, because it had its foundation on the rock. But everyone who hears these words of mine and does not put them into practice is like a foolish man who built his house on sand. The rain came down, the streams rose, and the winds blew and beat against that house, and it fell with a great crash."

 MATERIALS: Piece of tile or a large flat rock approximately 6" x 6"
Sand
Popsicle sticks (craft sticks)
Water
Buckets
A few rocks, 2" diameter

 IN ADVANCE: Choose an area of ground that slopes a little. When building the house on the sand foundation, keep the sticks loose for a more dramatic effect when the house falls down. The purpose of this activity is to demonstrate the passage of scripture. Do not use so much force and water that you knock down both houses. You may want to put a few rocks inside the house built on the tile to provide additional stability.

Words that are written in **bold** are when you, the parent, are speaking. Feel free to use your own words.

Big Idea

As Christians we live life by following the words of God and Jesus as written in the Bible. When we want to know how God wants us to treat others, what to do with our money, and what to do with our time, then we look at the Bible. The Bible is the foundation for how we live.

What is a foundation? The base of something. **Our house has a foundation: the part that holds up the rest of our house.**

Jesus tells us in the book of Matthew that families who follow the Bible will have a strong foundation for their lives. Jesus also says that those who do not follow the Bible will have a weak foundation for their lives.

Activity

Using these craft sticks, we are going to build two houses. Start building the houses as you continue to talk about the Bible story. You will also build two foundations for these houses and then try to wash away the foundations to see what happens.

Jesus says that families who follow the Bible are like those who build a house on rock. The rock represents a solid foundation. The rock also refers to Jesus. When a storm comes the rain, rising stream, and wind will not knock the house down. The storm represents hard times in life— when things don't go the way we hope.

Jesus says that families who do not follow the Bible are like those who build a house on sand. The sand represents a weak foundation. When a storm comes the rain, rising stream, and wind will knock the house down.

We are going to build a foundation of rock for one of our houses and a foundation of sand for the other house. Then we are going to see what happens when a river of water floods the houses.

Build a foundation using rocks and tiles and a foundation using sand. Pour water from the bucket and flood the foundations. See which house stands and which one falls.

Application

We are a Christian family who seeks to live life by God's Word—the Bible. In hard times—like the storm— we will remain standing like the house built on rock.

What are some principles we can learn from the Bible that will contribute to a strong foundation for our family? You might have children think on their own or use the following scriptures to help.

James 1:19-20 "Slow to become angry."

Philippians 2:14 "Do everything without complaining or arguing."

Proverbs 12:1 "He who hates correction is stupid."

Proverbs 6:23 "The corrections of discipline are the way to life."

Matthew 5:9 "Blessed are the peacemakers."

Romans 12:10 "Honor one another above yourselves."

1 Corinthians 13:5 "It (Love) is not rude, it is not self-seeking."

Lesson 2:
OUR VALUE

TEACHING GOAL: Our value comes from God.

1. Play theme song
2. Pray
3. Review last lesson
4. Lesson and discussion
5. Memorize: **God loves you; that's true value.**
6. Close in prayer

SCRIPTURE: Romans 5:8 "But God demonstrates his own love for us in this: While we were still sinners, Christ died for us."

John 3:16 "'For God so loved the world that he gave his one and only Son, that whoever believes in him shall not perish but have eternal life.'"

Psalm 8:5-7 "You made him a little lower than the heavenly beings and crowned him with glory and honor. You made him ruler over the works of your hands; you put everything under his feet: all flocks and herds, and the beasts of the field."

MATERIALS: Play money (ex. Monopoly money)
Candy, small toys (inexpensive from a dollar store)
Undesirable items like a piece of trash or an old shoe

Words that are written in **bold** are when you, the parent, are speaking. Feel free to use your own words.

Big Idea

What does the word "value" mean?
Worth in usefulness, importance, or desirability. **One way that we communicate value is by how much money it is worth. Using money as the guideline, what is the most valuable:**

Type of food: You may talk about a type of food like sushi or a particular expensive restaurant.

Which do people seem to value more, a teacher or a baseball player? Talk about how we pay some teachers $40,000 and some baseball players $25,000,000 a year.

Which rock do people value more, a diamond or piece of sandstone?

B> Activity

Today, I'm going to give you an opportunity to set the value on several items. First, you each get the same amount of play money. You will use this money to bid on a series of items. The person who bids the most for the item will get to keep the item.

I will show you eight different items on which you can bid. Without telling anyone else, you may want to decide which items are most important to you. Consider in advance how much of your money you are willing to spend on the items you want. If you spend all your money on the first item then you won't have anything left to bid on the other items.

Show everyone the auction items you have selected. (Choose six to eight items. Make sure one item is very desirable and another item has little if any value to the bidders.) Go through the process of holding up one item at a time and letting people bid. After all the bidding is done, discuss the experience. Who paid the most for which item? Which item was worth the least? Why did they bid on some items and not others? Did they bid more on an item than they originally planned? Did they get another item for less than they expected?

Sometimes we communicate how much we value things and people by how much money we spend. What are some other ways we communicate value? Time we spend with people. Love—our willingness to put the needs of someone else above our own needs.

 ## Application

How much does God value you and me? How did God set our value? Read Romans 5:8 and John 3:16. **God loves you so much that he sent his son Jesus to die for you. And look at the value we have in God's eyes.** Read Psalm 8:5-7. **God values us so much that he has put us in charge of everything he created. We are more important to God than the earth and animals. We are just a little lower than heavenly beings.**

Remember, your value does not come from how smart you are or how fast you run. It doesn't come from how popular you are. Your value comes from God—you are his child and he gave his son Jesus for you and made you more valuable than gold, silver, and diamonds (the earth).

Lesson 3:
THE TRINITY

 TEACHING GOAL: God, Jesus, and the Holy Spirit are one.

1. Play theme song
2. Pray
3. Review last lesson
4. Lesson and discussion
5. Memorize: **Three in one; God, Spirit, and Son.**
6. Close in prayer

 SCRIPTURE: Mark 1:10-11 "As Jesus was coming up out of the water, he saw heaven being torn open and the Spirit descending on him like a dove. And a voice came from heaven: 'You are my Son, whom I love; with you I am well pleased.'"

Matthew 28:19 "'Therefore go and make disciples of all nations, baptizing them in the name of the Father and of the Son and of the Holy Spirit.'"

 MATERIALS: Water
              Pan, lid
              Freezer, stove

Words that are written in **bold** are when you, the parent, are speaking. Feel free to use your own words.

 Big Idea

Tell the story of Jesus' baptism in Mark. **This is a special story because it shows Jesus the Son, the Holy Spirit in the form of a dove, and God the Father's voice from heaven, all in the same place at the same time.**

Have you ever had a bird land on you? Birds don't usually land on people, unless they are trained or controlled by someone. God the Father had the Holy

Spirit in the form of a dove descend and land on the shoulder of Jesus.

God, Jesus, and the Holy Spirit are one. The three in one is called the trinity. How can three things be one?

B▸ Activity

We can use water to help us learn about the trinity. The same item—water—comes in three different forms: water, ice, and steam. The water in this glass represents God. We are going to boil this glass of water and create steam. Let's say the steam represents the Holy Spirit. We are going to catch the steam in the lid and put it in the freezer, creating ice. Let's say the ice represents Jesus.

Take water and heat it to boiling on the stove, being careful to keep children a safe distance from the stove. Show how the water turns to steam. Use a metal pot lid and place it above the steam. (Use a potholder so the steam won't burn your hand and it demonstrates your respect for heat to the children.)

The pot lid will capture water droplets. Show the children how the steam turns back into water. Place the pot lid in the freezer. In a short time the water droplets will freeze. Scrape the ice off the lid and show the children that water turns to ice.

C▸ Application

Understanding God as Father, Son, and Holy Spirit is important for us in our Christian walk. We trust in God as the provider and controller of our lives and we usually pray to him. We trust in Jesus who understands our weaknesses and gives us confidence that we can come to him for anything. And we trust in the Holy Spirit to guide us and empower us to live each day. Take a moment and pray to God and talk to all three persons of the trinity and express your gratefulness.

Lesson 4:
TRAPS

 TEACHING GOAL: Jesus is our guide to get through the traps in life.

1. Play theme song
2. Pray
3. Review last lesson
4. Lesson and discussion
5. Memorize: **Trust Jesus to keep you free; from all the traps that he can see.**
6. Close in prayer

 SCRIPTURE: Joshua 23:12-13 Joshua warns his people to follow God's rules. If they do not follow God, but follow what others do, then they will find themselves ensnared and trapped.

 MATERIALS: Traps: rabbit trap (box, stick, and string), mouse trap, noose trap, sticky or fly trap, (optional: beaver trap)
Bait: cheese, carrots, scent
Blindfold
Tennis ball

Words that are written in **bold** are when you, the parent, are speaking. Feel free to use your own words.

Big Idea

Do you remember any of the stories of Joshua? Joshua and the battle of Jericho. Joshua crossing the Jordan River. Joshua, friend of Moses. **Joshua was the leader of the Israelites. When he got old and was about to die, he called the people together to tell them something special.**

Joshua warned them to follow God's rules, like the ten commandments. Do you know any of the ten commandments? God also warned his people, the Israelites, not to hang around with people who made bad choices. It is a "trap" to hang around people who sin (make bad choices).

Do you know what a trap is? Can you give an example of a trap? We are going to look at several traps. Before there were grocery stores, people hunted with traps to catch food.

▶ Activity

RABBIT TRAP: Set a box balanced on a stick. The stick has a string tied on the bottom. Place a carrot under the box and explain how the trap is used to catch rabbits. Roll a tennis ball under the trap, and the children can take turns pulling the string and trying to trap the ball.

NOOSE: Make a noose at the end of a rope. Put the noose down on the ground/floor. (The noose will work best if the rope pulls up and over a couch inside or tree limb outside.) Use some bait and talk about how the food attracted animals that would step into the noose. Each child can take a turn trapping Mom or Dad (explain how to pull the rope gently for the demonstration).

STICKY TRAP: Demonstrate using fake bugs or paper bugs how they get stuck in a sticky trap or on flypaper.

MOUSE TRAP: Demonstrate how a mouse trap works with cheese as bait. Use a pencil to trigger the trap. Keep children away from the trap.

(OPTIONAL) BEAVER TRAP: If you use a real beaver trap, then mark off an area to keep all children away from the trap. If the kids will not stay outside the marked area, then do not use this trap. Talk about the scent that trappers used to bait the beaver.

Joshua warned the Israelites, and God warns us about traps in life.

Adam and Eve were trapped. What was the bait? The tree of knowledge, the fruit. **What was the trap?** They wanted to do their own thing even though God told them not to. **What were the consequences?** They were kicked out of the Garden of Eden, and death.

Samson was trapped. What was the bait? Wanting to please Delilah. **What was the trap?** Cutting his hair. **What were the consequences?** He was captured by the Philistines and blinded.

Lot was trapped. What was the bait? The party life of Sodom and Gomorrah. **What was the trap?** Hanging out with people who lived in sin making bad choices. **What were the consequences?** Death.

What traps do we have to watch out for?

Lying is a trap. What is the bait? Avoiding trouble. **What are the consequences?** Leads to more lying and does not avoid trouble but creates more trouble.

Using bad words is a trap. What is the bait? Mad/hurt/selfish. **What are the consequences?** It hurts others and you can't take the words back.

Greed—wanting too many things is a trap. What is the bait? TV commercials, magazines, others' toys. **What are the consequences?** Wanting to take things that don't belong to you; spending money on yourself and not using it to help others. More things take more of your time.

 Application

Set up the traps in a room (with younger kids, you do not need to set the traps, but just place them on the floor). Blindfold each child one at a time. Spin them around a few times and tell them they have to cross the room, but they have two choices: they may try it themselves blindfolded or they may ask a parent, who is not blindfolded, to lead them across the room.

Our lives are full of traps. We can not see all of them until it is too late and we are caught. Jesus wants to be our guide, and if we follow him, he will keep us out of the traps. He can see traps that we cannot see.

Lesson 5:
DOUBTING THOMAS

 TEACHING GOAL: Believe in Jesus even when you can't see him.

1. Play theme song
2. Pray
3. Review last lesson
4. Lesson and discussion
5. Memorize: **Jesus promised a blessing for me; because I believe what I do not see.**
6. Close in prayer

 SCRIPTURE: John 20:24-29 "Now Thomas (called Didymus), one of the Twelve, was not with the disciples when Jesus came. So the other disciples told him, 'We have seen the Lord!' But he said to them, 'Unless I see the nail marks in his hands and put my finger where the nails were, and put my hand into his side, I will not believe it.' A week later his disciples were in the house again, and Thomas was with them. Though the doors were locked, Jesus came and stood among them and said, 'Peace be with you!' Then he said to Thomas, 'Put your finger here; see my hands. Reach out your hand and put it into my side. Stop doubting and believe.' Thomas said to him, 'My Lord and my God!' Then Jesus told him, 'Because you have seen me, you have believed; blessed are those who have not seen and yet have believed.'"

 MATERIALS: Quarter

Words that are written in **bold** are when you, the parent, are speaking. Feel free to use your own words.

 Big Idea

(Right before Family Time starts let everyone see you asking someone to let you borrow a quarter, or announce that you are picking up a quarter from the table. Stick the quarter in your pocket.) Reach in your pocket, make a fist around the quarter, and pull out your hand so that everyone can see your fist but not the quarter inside. Ask each person, **Do you believe I have a quarter in my hand? Why or why not?** Listen to answers. **Do you believe I have a million dollars in my hand? Why or why not?** Listen to answers. **Is there any evidence that I might have a million dollars in my hand?** Listen. **Is there any evidence that I might have a quarter in my hand?** Listen. Put your hand back in your pocket without showing the quarter. Leave the quarter in your pocket.

Evidence is key to believing in something you do not see.

Is there any evidence that I could have had a quarter in my hand? I saw you put a quarter in your pocket. I've seen you with quarters before. A quarter is not a lot of money for you so you probably have one.

Do you have faith in me enough to believe I had a quarter in my hand? Why or why not? Yes, you probably did. No, you're always tricking us so I can't be sure.

 Activity

Reach back into your pocket and pull out the quarter. This time keep your hand open and allow everyone to see the quarter. **Do you believe I have a quarter in my hand?** Listen. Yes. **Is there anything I can say that would convince you that I don't have a quarter in my hand?** Listen. Someone may try to argue or come up with a gimmick, which is okay. **Do you believe I have a million dollars in my hand?** Listen. No. **Is there anything that I can say that would convince you that I do have a million dollars in my hand?** Listen. No.

Some people try to say that there is no God because no one has ever seen God, much like the first time I pulled out my hand and no one saw the quarter. There was evidence that the quarter was in my hand. In the same way, there is a ton of evidence that even though we do not see God, he does exist: **creation, changed lives, the Bible, an internal sense of right and wrong** (add personal examples).

Some people, trying to be silly or find a loophole, might argue that the quarter is not really in my hand even when I show it to them. Someone might say, "It's not really in your hand." Or, "When I close my eyes I can't see the quarter so maybe it's not in your hand." Or, "It might be a fake quarter."

Seems silly? Well, God sent his son Jesus, who lived a sinless life. He performed huge miracles like feeding 5,000 people, raising a dead man back to life, and healing the blind and the lame. Jesus fulfilled every prophesy about God's coming Messiah and he did things only God could do, but still people didn't believe.

 ## Application

Thomas was a disciple of Jesus. He ate, walked, and lived with Jesus. He heard Jesus teach and saw the miracles. He heard Jesus say that he was going to have to die but not to worry because he would come back again. Yet, when people said, "Jesus is alive!" three days after he was crucified and buried in a tomb, Thomas said, "I don't believe it." In fact, Thomas said, "Unless I can put my finger in the nail holes in Jesus' hands, I won't believe it." A week after Thomas said those words, he was in a locked room with the other disciples. SURPRISE! Out of nowhere, Jesus appeared in the locked room and said to Thomas, "Put your finger in the hole in my hand. Stop doubting and believe!" Thomas shouted, "My Lord and my God." Seeing Jesus raised from the dead, Thomas believed.

Then Jesus said, "Because you have seen me, you have believed; blessed are those who have not seen and yet have believed."

Jesus was talking about us. We are the ones who have not seen him but still believe in him. There is a special blessing waiting for us!

I want you to know that, like Thomas, it is normal to doubt. From time to time we may wonder, is God really there? Was Jesus really his son? It's okay to have questions. Then, look at the evidence. Creation. Sense of right and wrong. Changed lives of Christians. And like Thomas believe.

Lesson 6:
TAKE OUT THE GARBAGE

TEACHING GOAL: Fill our home with the fragrant aroma of Christ.

1. Play theme song
2. Pray
3. Review last lesson
4. Lesson and discussion
5. Memorize: **Throw away sin; let God's fragrance in.**
6. Close in prayer (Pray for each person and the stinky area they identified as their specific challenge.)

SCRIPTURE: 2 Corinthians 2:14-15 "But thanks be to God, who always leads us in triumphal procession in Christ and through us spreads everywhere the fragrance of the knowledge of him. For we are to God the aroma of Christ among those who are being saved and those who are perishing."

Deuteronomy 5:7-21	**2 Corinthians 12:20**
2 Corinthians 4:2	**Galatians 5:20-23**
Matthew 15:19	

MATERIALS: Garbage bag for each participant
               30 pieces of newspaper
               Marker
               Spray can of fabric or air freshener
               Rotten meat or smelly garbage

IN ADVANCE: Write on each piece of newspaper a word from the stinky column in this activity. You can add words that describe challenges specific to your family. Pick an area of the house for each participant and put an equal number of newspaper pages in each area.

Words that are written in **bold** are when you, the parent, are speaking. Feel free to use your own words.

A Big Idea

Today we are going to talk about "fragrance." What does "fragrance" mean? Listen to answers. **Have you ever heard someone say, "That smelly garbage has a strong fragrance"? Fragrance is usually used to describe good or desirable smells, not bad smells. The opposite of fragrance is stinky, really stinky! In our Family Time today we are going to use our noses to learn about an important spiritual truth.**

B Activity

Ask one person to go into another room and spray one item with the fabric or air freshener. Be careful to follow directions and use the spray only on approved items. After the person has finished spraying the item, everyone can enter the room and try to identify the sprayed item. Were participants able to correctly identify the item? Did the smell start to drift into other areas of the room? Was it a pleasant smell?

Listen to the Bible as God describes Christians as the fragrance of Christ. Ask someone to read 2 Corinthians 2:14-15. **Our lives are to be filled with the fragrance of Christ. People are to see and hear the goodness that comes from Christ in our actions, words, and attitude.**

Unfortunately, our lives don't always smell like the positive fragrance of Christ. Sometimes our actions, words, and attitudes are stinky! Open the bag of stinky garbage and allow people to smell it. **We want to get the stinky garbage out of our lives and out of our homes.**

Give each participant a garbage bag. Assign them a room to clean up and have them collect in their garbage bags the newspaper on which is written stinky actions, words, and attitudes. When they get all the "newspaper garbage" out of their assigned area, have them bring it back to the table.

You probably noticed that there were words written on the newspaper pages. These words represent stinky behaviors and attitudes that the Bible warns us about. The words on the newspaper come from lists of bad behavior found in Deuteronomy, 2 Corinthians, Galatians, and Matthew. We are going to take turns pulling a piece of newspaper out of our garbage bag and reading the stinky word. Then we have to think of the fragrant activity that would be opposite to the stinky word. For example, if someone has the word "hate" on their newspaper, what is the opposite of hate? Love.

STINKY:	FRAGRANCE:
Idolatry	Worshipping the one and only God
Using the Lord's name in vain	Praising God
No rest	Taking rest (Sabbath)
Dishonoring your parents	Honoring your parents
Murder	Self-control, love
Adultery	Faithfulness, commitment
Stealing	Giving, honesty
False testimony	Tell the truth
Covetousness	Contentment
Hate	Love
Out of control anger	Self-control
Disruption	Peace
Demanding	Patient
Meanness	Kindness
Bad actions	Goodness
Undependable	Faithfulness
Hurting others	Gentleness
Selfishness	Unselfishness, giving
Fighting	Peace
Jealousy	Contentment
Division	Unity
Slander	Truth
Gossip	Quiet, self-control
Arrogance	Humility
Disorder	Order
Impurity	Purity

STINKY:

Sexual sin
Secret ways
Deception
Distortion of God's Word
Witchcraft
Discord
Drunkenness
Evil thoughts
Pride
Sarcasm
Greed
Whining

FRAGRANCE:

Self-control, purity, modesty
Openness
Honesty
Truth
Godliness
Unity
Sobriety
Godly thoughts
Humility
Straight talk
Sharing
Gratefulness

 Application

All right! Stuff these stinky items back into your garbage bags and let's get them out of the house! Take them to the garbage.

Each person has one particular stinky behavior or attitude with which they struggle. Let's each identify one stinky thing we need to work on and we'll pray for it at the end of Family Time. Adults, lead by example. Share the area where you struggle.

Lesson 7:
SPIRITUAL MEMORY INVENTORY

 TEACHING GOAL: God wants us to learn about him in our home.

1. Play theme song
2. Pray
3. Review last lesson
4. Lesson and discussion
5. Memorize: **As we go from room to room; thoughts of Jesus bloom and bloom.**
6. Close in prayer

 SCRIPTURE: Deuteronomy 6:5-9 "Love the LORD your God with all your heart and with all your soul and with all your strength. These commandments that I give you today are to be upon your hearts. Impress them on your children. Talk about them when you sit at home and when you walk along the road, when you lie down and when you get up. Tie them as symbols on your hands and bind them on your foreheads. Write them on the doorframes of your houses and on your gates."

 MATERIALS: Paper
Colored pens or pencils

 IN ADVANCE: With younger children, draw a floor plan of your home using simple squares, rectangles, etc. to designate different rooms and areas. For older children you may want to make this a part of the activity and have each family member draw a floor plan.

Words that are written in **bold** are when you, the parent, are speaking. Feel free to use your own words.

 Big Idea

God's plan for learning about Jesus and the Christian faith is to have teaching in the home. I'm going to read

a verse from the Bible and you tell me when and where we are to learn about the commandments of God.
Read Deuteronomy 6:5-7. Sit at home. Walk along the road. When you lie down. When you get up. Put symbols of the faith on your hands, forehead, and on the doors.

How could someone put symbols of the faith on their hands? Jewelry. WWJD (What Would Jesus Do) rings, bracelets, etc. **How could someone put a symbol of the faith on their forehead?** A hat with a Christian message.

 Activity

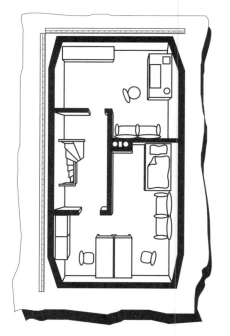

Show your family the floor plan you prepared in advance or ask each family member to make their own floor plan. Family members may want to write down their own answers or you may want to record the answers on one sheet. In the end you will want to have a list with everyone's answers. Start with a specific room and write the answers in that room on the floor plan.

We are going to talk about spiritual teaching in the home. Using this floor plan, let's make a list of spiritual memories from our home.

Define a spiritual memory and let kids know in advance that you may not accept all memories as spiritual memories. Acknowledge fun memories and talk about them but record only spiritual memories. There will be a tendency to take something fun or kind and tweak it to be a spiritual memory when that was not the intent at the time. For example, a child may say, "I picked up my clothes on the bedroom floor." This may be a spiritual lesson if you have specifically tied that task into a teaching on obedience, but in most cases it represents a daily chore.

Spiritual memories include conversations about our faith with other family members, friends, etc. It may have to do with a book, video, music, jewelry, or clothing with a spiritual message. Memories may include fixing meals for the sick, work for charities, meals with missionaries, or providing a room for someone in need. Bible studies and prayer are other memories to include.

OPTIONAL: You may want to provide an incentive for family members to think more deeply. You could give children a nickel or small piece of candy for each memory that makes the list.

 # Application

Talk about the memories and reinforce the lessons learned.

You may want to put something about the Christian faith on your wrist, forehead, or door frame. "WWJD" bracelets can be purchased at local Christian book stores inexpensively. You may want to make a poster to put on your bedroom door or just inside the door. Be creative!

Remember that Family Times create spiritual memories. Plan to conduct those times in various areas of your home.

Lesson 8:
MAKE TIME FOR REST

TEACHING GOAL: It is easy for our lives to get too busy. We need to make time for rest.

1. Play theme song
2. Pray
3. Review last lesson
4. Lesson and discussion
5. Memorize: **Give God your best; balance work and rest.**
6. Close in prayer

SCRIPTURE: Genesis 2:2 "By the seventh day God had finished the work he had been doing; so on the seventh day he rested from all his work."

Exodus 20:8 "'Remember the Sabbath day by keeping it holy.'"

Matthew 14:23 "After he had dismissed them, he went up on a mountainside by himself to pray. When evening came, he was there alone."

Ecclesiastes 4:6 "Better one handful with tranquillity than two handfuls with toil and chasing after the wind."

Psalm 46:10 "Be still, and know that I am God."

MATERIALS: 3 clear glasses, dirt, and a spoon

Words that are written in **bold** are when you, the parent, are speaking. Feel free to use your own words.

 Big Idea

Rest is important to God. It is so important that he included it as one of the ten commandments.

Rest is not just sleep. Rest is time to slow down from busy activities and listen to God. The Bible talks about sabbath. That means rest from activity.

God says, "Be still and know that I am God." Even God rested on the seventh day of creation from all his work to enjoy what he had created.

 Activity

Take clear glasses and fill them ¾ full of water. Add a teaspoon of dirt to the first glass and stir 10 times. Add two teaspoons of dirt to the second glass and stir 40 times. Add three teaspoons of dirt to the third glass and stir 100 times.

What happens to the water when we stir up the dirt? It gets cloudy, dirty. We can't see through it. **What happens to the water with more dirt and more stirring?** It's harder to see through. It is more cloudy and dirty. **How do we get clear water again?** We have to stop the stirring, and let the water rest. **After letting the glass of dirty water sit, the dirt starts falling to the bottom, and we can see through the water again. It takes longer for the water to get clear the more dirt we add and the more stirring we do.**

◖ Application

Let the kids do the activity again and this time explain:

The glass of water represents us. God wants us to take time to be still so that we can see clearly.

The dirt represents activity in our lives. It's okay to be active and have activity in our lives as long as we take time to rest so that we can listen to God and see clearly what activities we need to do.

Stirring represents how long we are active without taking a rest. Some people are always busy and do not rest. Sickness may be the only time when these people slow down.

Parents, give examples of quiet times when God talked to you. Set the example for your children by letting them see you take time to rest.

Lesson 9:
THREE BRAVE FRIENDS
PARENTAL SUPERVISION REQUIRED!

 TEACHING GOAL: In hard times, stand firm for God.

1. Play theme song
2. Pray
3. Review last lesson
4. Lesson and discussion
5. Memorize: **Do what is right; in God's sight.**
6. Close in prayer

 SCRIPTURE: Daniel 1 Daniel, Shadrach, Meshach, and Abednego take a stand to not eat from the king's table. God blesses all four.

Daniel 3 Shadrach, Meshach, and Abednego are thrown into the fire for not praying to the king's idol.

 MATERIALS: Corrugated cardboard and scissors
or utility knife
Gingerbread man template
Shallow dish
Clothes hanger (metal)
Three paper clips
2 ounces rubbing alcohol
(70% isopropyl)
1 ounce water
Matches or lighter
(Parent supervision required)
Tongs

NOTE: This activity will not work well outside because of the wind. It will work in the garage.

Words that are written in **bold** are when you, the parent, are speaking. Feel free to use your own words.

 **Big Idea**

In advance read Daniel 1 and Daniel 3. Start by telling the story from Daniel 1. Tell the story in your own words, highlighting the following key points:

DANIEL 1

- Daniel, Shadrach, Meshach, and Abednego were boys from royal families who had been captured and taken to another country called Babylon. These four boys were some of the few survivors of the war between the Israelites and Babylonians. Most of their friends and family members were most likely dead.
- King Nebuchadnezzar selected the four boys to receive a special education and special food. They had been treated as prisoners, and now they were being offered the best teaching and food in the country.
- Daniel thought it would go against their belief in God to eat the king's food, so he asked for permission not to eat it. Refusing to eat the king's food could have gotten Daniel and the other boys killed!
- God caused the Babylonian officials to show favor to the boys, and they were allowed to eat their special diet. God blessed them with strength and knowledge.

The four boys chose to do what was right even though they could be put in jail or even killed for disobeying the king. We are going to be talking about times at school and in our family when we may be tempted to do something wrong, but we need to do what is right and follow God.

Tell the story from Daniel 3 in your own words, highlighting the following key points:

DANIEL 3

- King Nebuchadnezzar made a 90-foot-high gold idol and commanded everyone to bow down and worship the idol. If people didn't bow down then they would be thrown into a fiery furnace.
- Shadrach, Meshach, and Abednego refused to bow down

and worship the idol. The boys said to the king, "O Nebuchadnezzar, we do not need to defend ourselves before you in this matter. If we are thrown into the blazing furnace, the God we serve is able to save us from it, and he will rescue us from your hand, O king. But even if he does not, we want you to know, O king, that we will not serve your gods or worship the image of gold you have set up." (Daniel 3:16-18)

- The king was furious and had the three boys thrown into the fiery furnace.
- The soldiers who threw the boys into the furnace were killed by the fire but Shadrach, Meshach, and Abednego were not burned or harmed.
- An angel joined the three boys in the fire.
- Nebuchadnezzar brought the boys out of the fire and said, "Praise be to the God of Shadrach, Meshach, and Abednego." Then the boys were promoted and given more honor in Babylon.

Again, the three boys chose to do what was right and follow God even though it meant they could be hurt or killed. The boys were not sure God would choose to save their lives. When we stand for what is right we might get hurt or God may choose to protect us.

▶ Activity

Cut out three "gingerbread cookie shaped" people from a piece of corrugated cardboard. Label the three cardboard-people Shadrach, Meshach, and Abednego. Prepare a solution that is 2 oz. rubbing alcohol (70% isopropyl) and 1 oz. water. Mix together well and put the solution on a shallow dish. Let the "people" soak in the solution. After mixing the alcohol and water move quickly before the alcohol evaporates.

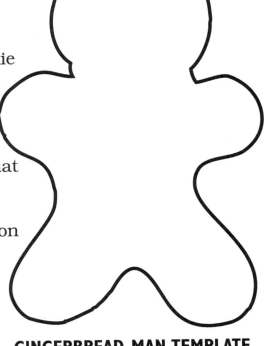

GINGERBREAD MAN TEMPLATE

Using the paper clips, attach the three wet cardboard-people to the hanger. Hold the top of the hanger with the tongs so that you can keep your body away from the fire. Remove any remaining alcohol solution and hold the hanger over a sink or safe area. Be sure to have water or a fire extinguisher close. **PARENTAL SUPERVISION REQUIRED.** Using a lighter, light the three cardboard-people. They will be consumed in fire but will not burn. Make sure the fire is out before touching the cardboard-people. The people will not be harmed by the fire.

This activity models the story of Shadrach, Meshach, and Abednego who were put in the furnace but thanks to God and his angel they were not harmed by the fire.

Application

The king told Daniel, Shadrach, Meshach, and Abednego to eat from the king's table but they refused because they believed God wouldn't want them to. Shadrach, Meshach, and Abednego also refused to bow down and worship the gold idol because they would only worship God.

In both cases the boys faced negative consequences for doing what was right. Think of some times when you may be asked to take a stand for God even if you might face negative consequences.

EXAMPLES:

Stand for What is Right	Negative Consequences
Friends your age are watching a movie that your parents won't let you see. You choose to obey your parents.	Kids laugh at you or say you're not "cool."
You break something important in your home. Instead of waiting for your parents to find out or denying that you were involved, you go to your parents and tell them what you did.	Your parents may be mad. You may have to replace the broken item.
You sit in a desk next to an unpopular girl at school. Instead of ignoring the girl, you talk with her and go out of your way to be nice.	Other kids laugh at you and may consider you to be unpopular.
You find out your friend doesn't go to church so you invite him to go with you to your youth group.	Other kids may make fun of you for going to church.

Look at our list. It can seem hard to take a stand but in most cases, it doesn't cost us much to do what is right. Compare our consequences to those facing Daniel, Shadrach, Meshach, and Abednego. Kids will laugh at us—they could have been thrown in jail. Kids may not think we are popular—they could have been burned in the furnace.

We need to keep in mind that it costs us very little to stand for God in our country. In other parts of the world, people are put in prison, hurt, or even killed for believing in God. We need to thank God for our freedom to be Christians and stand for God anytime we are given an opportunity.

Lesson 10:
SEEING SCRIPTURE

TEACHING GOAL: Seek to understand by visualizing scripture.

1. Play theme song
2. Pray
3. Review last lesson
4. Lesson and discussion
5. Memorize: **In scripture I see; God's message for me.**
6. Close in prayer

SCRIPTURE: Ephesians 3:17-18 "[I pray that] Christ may dwell in your hearts through faith. And I pray that you, being rooted and established in love, may have power, together with all the saints, to grasp how wide and long and high and deep is the love of Christ."

Colossians 2:6-7 "Continue to live in him, rooted and built up in him, strengthened in the faith as you were taught, and overflowing with thankfulness."

MATERIALS: Paper
Colored pencils
or crayons

IN ADVANCE: Type or print either Ephesians 3:17-18 or Colossians 2:7 on the top of a blank piece of paper. Larger sheets of paper will provide more room for the drawing activity. In the upper right corner of the paper make a list of key words from the passage:

EPHESIANS 3:17	COLOSSIANS 2:7
Christ	Roots
Home	Nourishment
Heart	Grow
Roots	Strong
Soil	Truth
Love	Overflow
God	Thanksgiving
Wide, long, high	Jesus

YOUNGER CHILDREN: Do the same as above using simple scriptures like Psalm 1:3, Genesis 1:20, or Luke 8:16.

Words that are written in **bold** are when you, the parent, are speaking. Feel free to use your own words.

 ## Big Idea

Sometimes I read the Bible and when I'm done I can't remember what I just read! The Bible is a book that needs to be studied. Sometimes we need to slow down our reading so we can listen and seek to understand what God is trying to tell us.

One way to slow down and understand the Bible better is to draw a picture of what we are reading. Each person is going to draw a picture of what they hear.

 ## Activity

Give each person a piece of paper with the scripture written at the top. Read the scripture together and point out the list of key words. **What do you picture in your mind when you hear this scripture?** Listen to their answers. **I want you to draw a picture of what you believe the verse is telling you. You can use the key words listed at the top of the paper or you can choose other images from the verse.**

Allow time for each person to draw a picture. If one person is taking more time than the others then you can stop him or her early and encourage this child to finish the picture later. Give children an opportunity to explain their pictures and what they believe the verse is saying.

 Application

Visualizing the scriptures is a good way to remember what they say. The next time you're sitting in church or listening to someone teach the Bible, take a few minutes and try to draw a picture of what they are saying to help you remember it.

Lesson 11:
PROMISE KEEPERS

 TEACHING GOAL: The Bible is filled with God's promises.

1. Play theme song
2. Pray
3. Review last lesson
4. Lesson and discussion
5. Memorize: **God's promises I keep; his blessings I will reap.**
6. Close in prayer: **Dear Jesus, thank you for this new game that will help us learn the four gospels, the fruit of the Spirit, and some of God's great promises for us.**

 SCRIPTURE: Psalm 33:4; Deuteronomy 31:6, John 14:26, Acts 2:21, John 14:2-3, Titus 1:2, Proverbs 3:5-6, and 2 Chronicles 7:14
(Scriptures are at the end of this activity.)

Galatians 5:22-23 "But the fruit of the Spirit is love, joy, peace, patience, kindness, goodness, faithfulness, gentleness and self-control. Against such things there is no law."

 MATERIALS: 8¹/₂" x 11" white paper (1 piece per person)
Photocopies of the Bible Promises page
Colored pens, pencils
Scissors
Glue stick or clear tape

Words that are written in **bold** are when you, the parent, are speaking. Feel free to use your own words.

 Big Idea

God's Word is full of promises. They are hidden all over the Bible. To illustrate this we want to play a game and

create a fun activity. As we do we'll be reminded that the promises of God are very helpful for our lives every day.

Can you think of the names of the gospels? We use that term "gospel" to describe the writings of four of the men in the Bible. Their names are Matthew, Mark, Luke, and John. Those books are all about Jesus and the gospel or good news that he came to bring us.

B▶ Activity

We are going to make "Promise Keepers." The first thing we are going to do is make the keepers. Follow instructions at the end of this activity. Parents may remember this game as "The Cootie Catcher."

The top of our Promise Keeper has four squares. Can you think of something from the Bible that involves the number four? The four gospels: Matthew, Mark, Luke, and John. **These are the four books that tell about the life of Jesus. Write the name of one gospel on each of the four top squares.** Adults may need to help younger children write the names.

The other side of our Promise Keeper has four large triangles, each divided by a crease, making eight small inner triangles. The book of Galatians (5:22-23) **gives us a list of nine characteristics that Christians are to demonstrate toward others. These characteristics are called fruit of the Spirit. Why do you think they are called fruit of the Spirit?** The "Spirit" refers to God's Holy Spirit that lives inside each Christian. "Fruit" refers to the list of characteristics. In the same way an apple tree has apple fruit, a Christian is to have love, joy, peace, etc. **Pick eight of the nine characteristics and write one on each of the eight triangles.**

FRUIT OF THE SPIRIT

Love	Joy	Peace	Patience
Kindness	Faithfulness	Gentleness	Self-Control
Goodness			

Open up each of the four inner triangle flaps with the fruit of the Spirit written on them. Under each flap there is room to tape or glue two of God's promises. Cut the promises from the Bible Promises page and tape or glue two under each of the four flaps.

Now we're ready to play. Demonstrate how to play the game. Work your fingers into the four corners of the keeper. With the sections closed, ask someone to pick one of the gospels. For example, if they pick "Mark" then open and close the keeper so that alternating fruit of the Spirit show as you say each letter M-A-R-K. Stop on the last letter with the keeper open. Ask your partner to pick one fruit of the Spirit that is showing inside the keeper. For example, if they pick "Peace" then open and close the keeper as you say each letter P-E-A-C-E. Stop on the last letter with the keeper open. Once again, your partner picks a fruit of the Spirit. For example, let's say they pick "Joy." This time you open up the inner triangle flap and read the Bible promise under the word "Joy."

Take turns and repeat the game.

INSTRUCTIONS FOR MAKING A "PROMISE KEEPER"

Take an 8½" x 11" sheet of paper.

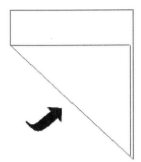

Fold corner up until it meets the other side.

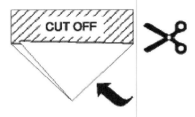

Fold other corner up until it meets the other side—then cut off the rectangle at the top.

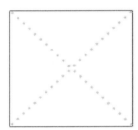

Unfold it. You should now have an 8½" x 8½" piece.

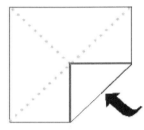

Fold up all four corners so that the points meet in the middle.

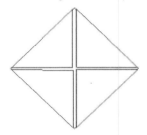

It should now look like this. Flip it over.

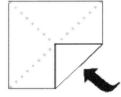

Fold up all four corners so that the points meet in the middle. Turn it over.

It should now look like this. (This is how it looks turned over.)

Now fold the top back.

Work your fingers into the four corners from the fold side—work the creases to form the four points.

BIBLICAL PROMISES

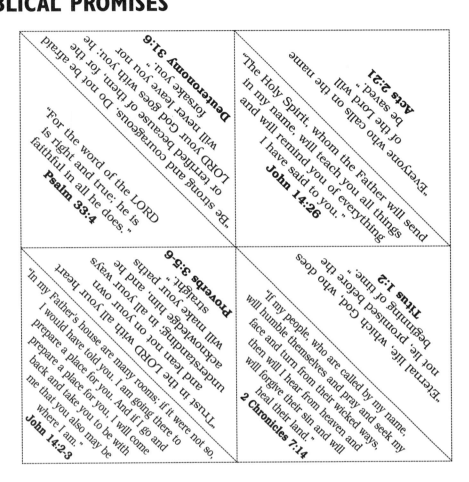

"The Holy Spirit, whom the Father will send in my name, will teach you all things and will remind you of everything I have said to you."
John 14:26

"Everyone who calls on the name of the Lord will be saved."
Acts 2:21

"Be strong and courageous. Do not be afraid or terrified because of them, for the LORD your God goes with you; he will never leave you, nor forsake you."
Deuteronomy 31:6

"For the word of the LORD is right and true; he is faithful in all he does."
Psalm 33:4

"If my people, who are called by my name, will humble themselves and pray and seek my face and turn from their wicked ways, then will I hear from heaven and will forgive their sin and will heal their land."
2 Chronicles 7:14

"Eternal life, which God, who does not lie, promised before the beginning of time,"
Titus 1:2

"Trust in the LORD with all your heart and lean not on your own understanding; in all your ways acknowledge him, and he will make your paths straight."
Proverbs 3:5-6

"In my Father's house are many rooms; if it were not so, I would have told you. I am going there to prepare a place for you. And if I go and prepare a place for you, I will come back and take you to be with me that you also may be where I am."
John 14:2-3

Application

Reading the Bible is like a treasure hunt.
As we read it we often stumble
across these and many
other promises of God.
Let's take a moment and
pray and thank God for
giving us so many
promises in
the Bible for
our lives.

Lesson 12:
PRAY FOR THE PRESIDENT

TEACHING GOAL: Pray for those in authority.

1. Play theme song
2. Pray
3. Review last lesson
4. Lesson and discussion
5. Memorize: **God, we pray; for the president today.**
6. Close in prayer

SCRIPTURE: Romans 13:1-2 "Everyone must submit himself to the governing authorities, for there is no authority except that which God has established. The authorities that exist have been established by God. Consequently, he who rebels against the authority is rebelling against what God has instituted, and those who do so will bring judgment on themselves."

1 Timothy 2:1-2 "I urge, then, first of all, that requests, prayers, intercession and thanksgiving be made for everyone—for kings and all those in authority."

2 Chronicles 7:14 "If my people, who are called by my name, will humble themselves and pray and seek my face and turn from their wicked ways, then will I hear from heaven and will forgive their sin and will heal their land."

MATERIALS: Pen, paper, envelope, postage stamps Newspaper or news magazine

Words that are written in **bold** are when you, the parent, are speaking. Feel free to use your own words.

Big Idea

Read the scriptures listed above or put them into your own words. **The Bible tells us to pray for those in authority and for those in government.**

 **Activity**

Today we are going to write a letter to the President of the United States. We are going to write down our prayers, mail them to him, and let him know we are praying for him. Adults may need to write down the prayer for younger children. Younger children may also want to color pictures to be included with the prayer.

IDEAS TO INCLUDE IN YOUR PRAYER:
- Include the verse from 1 Timothy with your prayer.
- Look at the newspaper/news magazine and include prayer on current events.
- Pray for wisdom, justice, peace.

MAILING ADDRESS: "Name", President
The White House
1600 Pennsylvania Ave.
Washington, DC 20500

 Application

Let's take a moment and read our prayers to God for our president. Each person can take a turn offering a prayer to God by reading what's written on his or her paper.

Lesson 13:
PEER PRESSURE

 TEACHING GOAL: God's Word will guide you to make the right decisions even when friends tempt you to do what you know is wrong.

1. Play theme song
2. Pray
3. Review last lesson
4. Lesson and discussion
5. Memorize: **When we hear tempting from our friends' voices; with God's help we can still make good choices.**
6. Close in prayer

 SCRIPTURE: Proverbs 1:8-10 "Listen, my son, to your father's instruction and do not forsake your mother's teaching. They will be a garland to grace your head and a chain to adorn your neck. My son, if sinners entice you, do not give in to them."

 MATERIALS: Jar
String
Fan or hair dryer
2 heavy washers or some type of small weight

Words that are written in **bold** are when you, the parent, are speaking. Feel free to use your own words.

 Big Idea

The Bible contains advice from a father to his child. King David had a son named Solomon. Solomon wrote this advice, called Proverbs, to his son. The father gives his son advice to help him live a peaceful life that will be pleasing to God. Read Proverbs 1:8-10.

King Solomon tells his son that there are people who will try to tempt him into doing wrong.

B▶ Activity

Set a jar on the floor. Using a 2-foot piece of string, allow each child to stand and take a turn guiding the string into the jar. **Being able to get the string into the small jar opening represents making the right choice, doing what is right, or being obedient. Should you jump on the bed? The answer is "no" and when you don't jump on the bed, it is the right choice and you are being obedient, like putting the string in the jar.**

Turn on the fan (or hair dryer) next to the top of the jar or have everyone except the person holding the string blow on the string. Now allow each child to stand and try to put the string in the jar. The wind will make it impossible to get the string in the jar. **The wind represents peer pressure, like friends telling you to do something when you know it is wrong. They make it hard to do the right thing, or to be obedient.**

Tie the weights onto the end of the string. **The weights represent God's Word and our relationship with Jesus. Our relationship with Jesus and his instruction in the Bible tells us what is right to do. In Proverbs, God says to listen to the rules of our parents and not to be tempted by those people who tell us to make wrong choices. Even with the wind blowing, the weight helps guide the string into the jar. Just like the washer on the end of the string helped guide the string into the jar, Jesus will help you to obey your parents and follow the rules, even if you have friends telling you to do the wrong thing.**

◆ Application

When the person who is tempting you to do wrong is a friend, it is called "peer pressure." In fact, you may sometimes tempt your friends to make bad choices and when you do that, the Bible says it is sin and it is wrong. Here are some examples:

1. When your friends come over and they want you to jump on the bed, and you know it is wrong, but you do it anyway—that is being tempted by friends, and that is peer pressure.

What might you do to not get blown by peer pressure in this situation?

2. When your friends come over and tell you to exclude your little brother or sister from a game, and you know that isn't kind, but you do it anyway—that is being tempted by friends to make a bad choice, and that is peer pressure.

What might you do to not get blown by peer pressure in this situation?

3. When your friends come over and want to play with dad's computer, and you have been told not to, but you let them—that is being tempted by friends, and that is peer pressure.

What might you do to not get blown by peer pressure in this situation?

4. When you go to your friend's house and you tell her to get a snack even though her mother has told her not to, but she does anyway because you asked her—that is tempting your friend, and that is peer pressure.

What might you do to not blow your friend with peer pressure in this situation?

5. When you go to your friend's house and you watch a TV show that your friend's mother has told you not to—that is tempting your friend, and that is peer pressure.

What might you do to not blow your friend with peer pressure in this situation?

Lesson 14:
CHRISTMAS FUTURE

TEACHING GOAL: God revealed his plans to prophets, who then foretold the birth of Jesus hundreds of years before he was born.

1. Play theme song
2. Pray
3. Review last lesson
4. Lesson and discussion
5. Memorize: **Of the birth of Jesus the prophets told us. The words came true; God's Word we trust.**
6. Close in prayer

SCRIPTURE: Isaiah 9:6 (prediction: Christ's birth) "For to us a child is born, to us a son is given, and the government will be on his shoulders. And he will be called Wonderful Counselor, Mighty God, Everlasting Father, Prince of Peace."

Isaiah 7:14 (prediction: born of a virgin) "Therefore the Lord himself will give you a sign: The virgin will be with child and will give birth to a son, and will call him Immanuel."

Micah 5:2 (prediction: born in Bethlehem) "'But you, Bethlehem Ephrathah, though you are small among the clans of Judah, out of you will come for me one who will be ruler over Israel, whose origins are from of old, from ancient times.'"

MATERIALS: Paper
Pencil
"Prediction" cards

IN ADVANCE: Practice solving the two activities, "Predicting the Answer" and "Knowing Your Thoughts." Explanations on how to do the two activities are included with this lesson. Practice until you are familiar with the solutions and you can do them smoothly.

Words that are written in **bold** are when you, the parent, are speaking. Feel free to use your own words.

Big Idea

What is a "prophet"? Someone who predicts the future. **God revealed to prophets hundreds of events that were yet to happen. These revelations are called prophecies. Did you know the Bible is full of prophecies concerning Jesus? His birth was predicted hundreds of years before it happened.**

Activity

Let's play a game and see if I can "predict" the answer to a very big math problem. I'll predict the answer and write it down. Use the "Predicting the Answer" explanation to reach your prediction. Repeat with each child.

Let's try another activity where I can guess what you are thinking. Choose a number between 1-31 and using the five cards I will be able to predict your number. Use the "Knowing Your Thoughts" explanation and cards to reach your prediction. Repeat with each child.

Application

These two activities were just simple math tricks. There was no actual "predicting" involved at all. However, when God revealed his plans to his prophets, they were not simple math tricks. In many cases the prophets gave their prophecies hundreds of years before the event took place. The birth of Jesus is one of these predictions. Let's read about three of these predictions. Read the verses.

Discuss how God had a plan for the birth of his son since the beginning of time. **The birth of Jesus is truly a miraculous event. As we celebrate Christmas this year, let's not forget how miraculous it was that Jesus' birth was predicted hundreds of years in advance.**

Predicting the Answer

DIRECTIONS

1. If the child is not old enough to do math, an adult or older child will need to help with the addition.

2. Have the child write a 5 digit number on a piece of paper. Hint: If the last number is less than 2, you will need to use the principle of borrowing in your addition.

3. Make your prediction by doing the following. (Let the children see you writing something down but do not reveal your answer until the end.)

   Subtract 2 from the child's number so that it becomes a completely new number. Write down the new number on a separate piece of paper.

   Write the number 2 at the front of the new 5 digit number you just wrote. The new 6 digit number will be the answer to the problem.

EXAMPLES:	A.	B.	C.
Child's number:	63789	63781	60000
Subtract 2 from the last number	63787	63779	59998
Write the number 2 at the front of the list	263787	263779	259998

The last number in this process will be the number you write down as your prediction.

The child has written down the first number. You have written down and hidden your prediction. Now, have the children follow the directions below. (I will use example A above to show what the children need to do.)

4. Have the child write a random row of 5 numbers below their first row
    Row 1 (child)   63789
    Row 2 (child)   35973

5. Now you write a row of numbers, supposedly random, however each number in your row and the row the child just wrote must equal 9.
    Row 1 (child)   63789
    Row 2 (child)   35973
    Row 3 (YOU)   64026
    Each digit in row 2 and 3 must equal 9 when added

6. Have the child add one more row of random numbers and you will again add another row, making sure digits in row 4 and row 5 equal 9.
    Row 1 (child)   63789
    Row 2 (child)   35973
    row 2 and 3 individual digits equal 9
    Row 3 (YOU)   64026
    Row 4 (child)   47568
    Row 4 and 5 individual digits equal 9
    Row 5 (YOU)   52431
    _____

    Add total   263787 = Your prediction of 263787

7. Add the numbers. Reveal your "prediction" and the numbers will match.

Knowing Your Thoughts

DIRECTIONS

Have a child choose a number between 1-31. They do not tell you the number. One at a time, show the child each of the 5 cards.

Ask the child, **Do you see your number on this card?**
If the child answers "yes," make a mental note of the number directly beneath the tree trunk (3rd number, top row).

Mentally add the numbers directly under the trees from the cards in which the child says "yes," when you ask if their number is on the card. If the child says "no" add a "0." The total of the numbers you will add will equal the number the child picked. As soon as you show all 5 cards tell the child what their number is. You will need to pay attention to their answers and quickly add in your head, so that it seems spontaneous.

EXAMPLE: The child picks the number 17. They say "yes" to card number 1 (number below the tree is a 1) and number 5 (number below tree is 16). There are only two cards with the number 17 (1 +16) so all the other cards are 0.

Cut out a copy of the prediction cards.

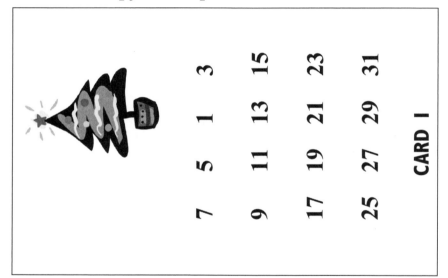

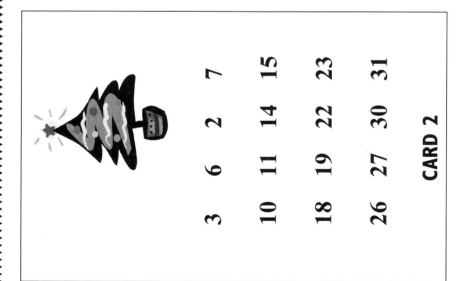

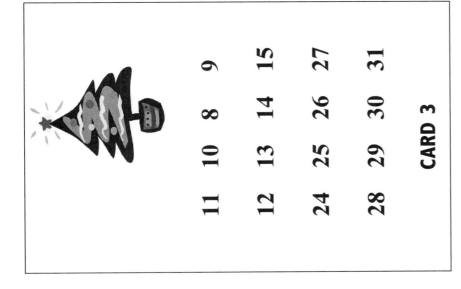

11 10 8 9
12 13 14 15
24 25 26 27
28 29 30 31

CARD 3

5 6 4 7
12 13 14 15
20 21 22 23
28 29 30 31

CARD 4

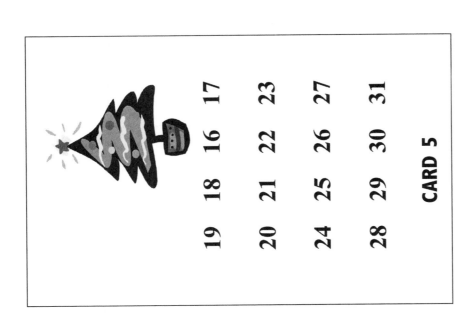

19 18 16 17
20 21 22 23
24 25 26 27
28 29 30 31

CARD 5

Lesson 15:
CHAINS

TEACHING GOAL: Being a Christian may be unpopular, but that's okay.

1. Play theme song
2. Pray
3. Review last lesson
4. Lesson and discussion
5. Memorize: **Remember the pains; of Christians in chains.**
6. Close in prayer

SCRIPTURE: Ephesians 6:19-20 "Pray also for me, that whenever I open my mouth, words may be given me so that I will fearlessly make known the mystery of the gospel, for which I am an ambassador in chains."

Colossians 4:18 "I, Paul, write this greeting in my own hand. Remember my chains."

MATERIALS: Paper gum wrappers (approximately 20 per bracelet)
Pen, pencil, or colored pencils
MORE INFO:
www.biblicalparenting.org/gumjewelry.asp
(folding gum wrapper picture)
MORE INFO: www.persecution.com
(countries where Christians are persecuted)

Words that are written in **bold** are when you, the parent, are speaking. Feel free to use your own words.

 Big Idea

Sometimes it is unpopular to be a Christian. Can you think of times when it has been difficult to stand up for Jesus or live the way Jesus tells us to live? Listen and share your own experiences. **People were angry and didn't like Paul, the apostle. Several times he was put in prison. While he was in prison he wrote letters to the churches he helped to start.** Read Ephesians 6:19 and Colossians 4:18. **Paul was in jail not because he killed someone, not because he stole, not because he lied, but because he told people the truth about Jesus.**

We are blessed to live in a country where we can talk about Jesus and go to church without being put in jail. But many people in the world do not have this freedom. In some countries people are beaten, imprisoned, and even killed because they talk about Jesus.

B Activity

We are going to make "chain bracelets" to remember the experiences of Paul the apostle and to remember those Christians today who live under persecution.

MAKING GUM WRAPPER CHAIN BRACELETS
Follow the instructions below and located at www.biblicalparenting.org/gumjewelry.asp to make each person a chain bracelet. You may want to turn the paper inside out so the white part of the gum wrapper is showing. On each wrapper write the name of a country where Christians are being persecuted.

Use the colored paper wrapper that surrounds the inner wrapper on individual pieces of gum inside a pack of gum:

1. Fold the gum wrapper in half, lengthwise, creating a center fold line. Rip in half along the length.

2. Fold in half along length. Open and fold both edges to the center. Crease.
3. Fold in half lengthwise, with the edges inside.
4. Fold in half, widthwise, creating a center fold line.
5. Open and fold both ends into the center fold line.
6. Fold in half on fold line created in #4.
7. Repeat steps 1 to 6 with all of your wrappers. To make a chain, link your wrappers together, as follows: Each link has two 'arms.' One edge of each arm is folded and the other edge is 'leafed.' It's easier to work with the folded side when connecting your links. Slip the arms of each link into the folded slots of the previous link. When you put the first two links together, your chain will have an 'L' shape. The third link should go in the opposite direction and the fourth link will make your chain look like a 'W.' Continue adding links. Slip the last link into the slots of the first link and tape it in place with Scotch tape.

▶ Application

COUNTRIES WHERE CHRISTIANS ARE PERSECUTED

Afghanistan	Algeria	China	Colombia	Cuba
Ethiopia	India	Indonesia	Iran	Iraq
Libya	North Korea	Syria	Tajikistan	Vietnam

When we wear these bracelets it will remind us to pray for Christians who live in countries where they are persecuted. Each time you put it on or take it off, say a prayer for Christians who are in jail and suffer because they believe in Jesus. Also, thank God that we live in a country where we can talk freely about Jesus.

Lesson 16:
WEB OF LOVE

 TEACHING GOAL: God calls us to hold each other up with love.

1. Play theme song
2. Pray
3. Review last lesson
4. Lesson and discussion
5. Memorize: **Honor God above; build a web of love.**
6. Close in prayer

SCRIPTURE: Matthew 22:39 "'Love your neighbor as yourself.'"

Matthew 5:44 "Love your enemies and pray for those who persecute you."

John 13:35 "'By this all men will know that you are my disciples, if you love one another.'"

 MATERIALS: Large ball of yarn, made of 2 or 3 skeins
Balloon and marker
Paper and pen

NOTE: This activity works best with six to ten people. You may want to do this activity with another family.

Words that are written in **bold** are when you, the parent, are speaking. Feel free to use your own words.

Big Idea

Read out loud the three short verses listed above. **Jesus tells us to love others: our neighbors, our family, our friends, our classmates, even people we don't like very much.**

We are going to begin by making a list of things we can do to show that we care and that we love our friends, our neighbors, our classmates, people we may not like, and even people we do not know. Take a few minutes and make your list of "loving and caring" actions. You will need at least 20 items on your list to successfully complete the activity.

B▶ Activity

Inflate the balloon and tie a knot in the end. Draw a face on the balloon with the marker. **This balloon represents a person. The person may be a family member, friend, classmate, neighbor, enemy, or someone we don't even know. We are going to need our balloon person later in the activity.**

Form a circle by holding out your arms and touching finger tips. Drop your hands. You are ready to create a Web of Love. The leader begins with the ball of yarn. Hold onto the end of the yarn and toss the ball back and forth to people in the circle. It works best if you unroll a little slack of yarn before tossing the ball. Show the children how to unroll some slack before tossing the ball.

This circle of people that we have created represents our neighborhood, school, church, city, even people we do not know around the world. We are going to create a Web of Love using the ideas that we wrote down at the beginning of the activity. I will say an idea from our list of caring and loving ideas then toss the ball to someone else in the circle. When you get the ball of yarn, loop the yarn around your finger (or waist) then say an idea from our list and toss the ball to someone else in the circle. It is okay to repeat ideas if you have the same idea as someone else.

Toss the ball of yarn back and forth SIX times and then stop. **We'll continue in a minute. Let's put our balloon person in the middle of our circle. Bounce him up and down with the yarn web and let's see if we have shown enough love to keep him from falling through the web.** Do this a few times, allowing the balloon to fall through and hit the ground. **Looks like we need more love webbing! Let's come up with some more ideas and keep tossing the yarn back and forth.** Stop again after TWELVE tosses and try to keep the balloon up. Try to come up with as many different ideas as you can.

Stop after TWENTY tosses and put the balloon in the middle again. As you bounce the balloon around, talk about what you have learned.

OPTIONAL: Have everyone take one or two steps in toward the center of the circle until your shoulders are touching. As you move in, pull the slack out of the web so that the yarn remains tight. **How does the web change when we become closer? Is it easier to keep the balloon person from falling? What could we do to be closer with our family, neighbors, and friends?**

 Application

Each person think of one thing they can do this week in the home, neighborhood, at church, or at school to create a Web of Love for other people.

Lesson 17:
KNOCK SIN OUT OF OUR LIVES

TEACHING GOAL: We need Jesus to take our sin away so we can be back together with God.

1. Play theme song
2. Pray
3. Review last lesson
4. Lesson and discussion
5. Memorize: **Jesus knocks our sin away; so close to God we can stay.**
6. Close in prayer

SCRIPTURE: Romans 3:23 "For all have sinned and fall short of the glory of God."

Hebrews 4:15 "We have one [Jesus] who has been tempted in every way, just as we are—yet was without sin."

1 John 5:17 "All wrongdoing is sin."

MATERIALS: Glass jar with wide mouth, filled with water
Aluminum pie pan
Paper and pen
Cardboard toilet paper tube
Egg, raw or hard boiled
Masking tape
Broom

Words that are written in **bold** are when you, the parent, are speaking. Feel free to use your own words.

A Big Idea

Talk about sin. **Sin is doing wrong things** (1 John 5:17). **All of us have sinned (done wrong things)** (Romans 3:23). **All have sinned except whom?** Jesus was without sin (Hebrews 4:15).

What wrong things did the following people do? Write them on pieces of paper and put them in the pie pan.

Adam and Eve   Pilate
Goliath   Pharaoh
Belshazzar   Lot
Judas

What wrong things do we do? Write them on pieces of paper and put them in the pie pan.

Using bad words   Lying
Hitting   Stealing
Disobeying   Being selfish

What can we do to help us do more good things and fewer wrong things? Write them on pieces of masking tape and put them on the broom handle.

Believe in Jesus   Go to church
Obey parents   Read the Bible
Pray   Go to Sunday School
Have Family Times   Say "no" to doing bad things

 **Activity**

Place the jar filled with water near the edge of a table. Put the pieces of paper listing the sins in the pie plate and place it on top of the jar. Center the toilet paper tube vertically on the pie plate, also being careful to ensure the tube is centered over the jar opening under the pie plate. Place the egg sideways, balanced on top of the tube. Place the jar in a position so that only the edge of the pie plate sticks out over the edge of the table.

In this activity we start with a pie pan and some pieces of paper. The pieces of paper represent sins in our lives. Sins are bad choices that we make, choices that God would not want us to make. Use the pieces of paper that have sins written on them. **The jar of water represents**

people, you and me. The egg represents God. If we are the jar of water and God is the egg then what separates us from God? Sin. **What we need is a sin buster. We need someone who can come into our lives and take the sin away so that we can be back together with God. Who do you think can be our sin buster?** Jesus. **That's right! Jesus represented by the broom is our sin buster.** Write Jesus on a piece of masking tape and put it around the top of the broom.

Stand the broom next to the table. While holding back the broom handle, step on the straw part of the broom. Only the pie pan should hang over the edge of the table. Press down on the table with your free hand next to the jar. (This adds extra support.) Pull back the broom handle and release. The broom should act as a "spring." The broom will knock the pie pan out of the middle. The table will stop the momentum of the broom handle and the egg will fall down into the water. **When Jesus knocks the sin out of our lives, we can be back together with God.**

 Application

God wants us to understand the concept of forgiveness. When Jesus died on the cross for us, he made it possible for our sins to get knocked out of the picture. That happens when we trust Jesus in our lives. He comes into our hearts and provides forgiveness in our lives.

That forgiveness isn't just for the past sins. It's even for any future sins we'll commit. Now that's quite a sin buster!

Lesson 18:
CREATION

TEACHING GOAL: God planned the creation of our universe.

1. Play theme song
2. Pray
3. Review last lesson
4. Lesson and discussion
5. Memorize: **God spoke and all we see; was created and came to be.**
6. Close in prayer

SCRIPTURE: Genesis 1:1 "In the beginning God created the heavens and the earth."

Genesis 1 Story of creation.

Romans 1:20 "For since the creation of the world God's invisible qualities—his eternal power and divine nature—have been clearly seen, being understood from what has been made, so that men are without excuse."

Colossians 1:16-17 "For by him all things were created: things in heaven and on earth, visible and invisible, whether thrones or powers or rulers or authorities; all things were created by him and for him. He is before all things, and in him all things hold together."

MATERIALS: Mystery Square and answer sheet (provided)
Alphabet letters (provided)
Pencil

IN ADVANCE: Cut out the letters on the "Alphabet Letters" sheet.

Words that are written in **bold** are when you, the parent, are speaking. Feel free to use your own words.

A Big Idea

Did you know that some people think that the world came together without a plan? They think everything just happened. The Bible tells us that "in the beginning God created the heavens and the earth." It didn't just happen. It took God's plan.

Tell the story of creation in your own words. Read Romans 1:20 and Colossians 1:16-17. **God took what wasn't seen, the invisible, and created our whole universe. Romans 1:20 tells us that because of what we can see through his creation, we have no excuse for not believing in God. How do you think you would feel if you made a beautiful statue with clay, spent time planning it and making it, then people said it just appeared that way?** Sad. **How do you think it makes God feel to have people say, "It all just happened and evolved into what it is today"?** Sad too.

B Activity

Let's try an experiment with this pile of alphabet letters. **Take turns throwing all the letters into the air and when they fall down they are going to spell your name.** Let child toss up the letters. As they fall, act confused that a name didn't appear. **Let's try it again** (unsuccessfully). **I wonder what's wrong. Maybe it's just your name. Let's try it with someone else's name.** Try again with other children or yourself. **I really want this to work and I can't understand why it won't. What do you think we need to do to get the letters to spell one of our names?** You can't do it by throwing them in the air. You must do it yourself, spelling out the name. **Why do we have to spell it out?** We need to think and follow a plan to spell a name.

Show the Mystery Square with the blank spaces to the children. **There are 3 numbers in each row (in any direction) and one blank square. Pick a row, column, or even a diagonal row. Add them together and you**

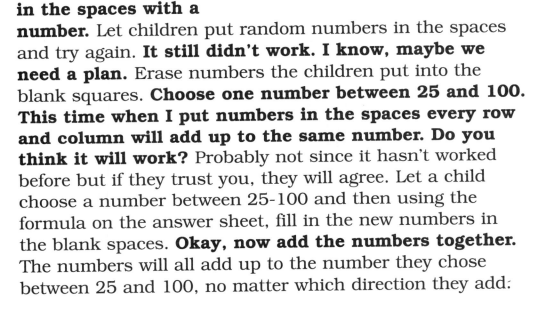

will get the same answer every time. Try it. You may need to help younger children, or omit this activity if your child is too young. Children will find that it doesn't work. It is supposed to work. I wonder what went wrong. Maybe we need to fill in the spaces with a number. Let children put random numbers in the spaces and try again. It still didn't work. I know, maybe we need a plan. Erase numbers the children put into the blank squares. Choose one number between 25 and 100. This time when I put numbers in the spaces every row and column will add up to the same number. Do you think it will work? Probably not since it hasn't worked before but if they trust you, they will agree. Let a child choose a number between 25-100 and then using the formula on the answer sheet, fill in the new numbers in the blank spaces. Okay, now add the numbers together. The numbers will all add up to the number they chose between 25 and 100, no matter which direction they add.

 ## Application

This puzzle is called a Mystery Square. It took someone's mind to plan it, to make it work. Someone was very smart to figure it out. It's a mystery to us because we don't understand it. Our world is the same way. Just like the Mystery Square, the creation of the world may be a mystery to us but it is not a mystery to the creator—God.

Lesson 18

ALPHABET LETTERS

A	A	A	A	A	B	B	B	B	C
C	C	C	C	D	D	D	D	E	E
E	E	E	E	F	F	F	F	G	G
G	G	H	H	H	H	I	I	I	I
I	J	J	J	J	K	K	K	K	L
L	L	L	L	M	M	M	M	N	N
N	O	O	O	O	P	P	P	Q	Q
R	R	R	R	S	S	S	S	T	T
T	T	T	U	U	U	U	V	V	V
W	W	W	W	X	X	X	Y	Y	Y
Y	Z	Z	Z	A	B	C	D	E	F

MYSTERY SQUARE

4	5	11	
	10	8	1
6	3		12
9		2	7

1. Choose a number between 25-100
2. Using the "N" formula below, calculate "N"
3. For each empty space on the Mystery Square, the answer sheet has an additional calculation (N, N+1, N-1, N+2). Make this additional calculation and fill in each empty space.
4. Add four numbers in any direction and it will equal the number you originally chose in step #1.

N FORMULA: N = chosen number (the number chosen between 25-100) minus 20

EXAMPLE:

1. Randomly chosen number: 77
2. Calculate N: 77-20 = 57, N=57
3. Additional calculations: a) Row 1, square 4: N=57, b) Row 2, square 1: 57+1=58, c) Row 3, square 3: 57-1=56, d) Row 4, square 2: 57+2=59. Fill in each empty space with these totals.
4. Add a row in any direction and it will equal 77 (i.e. Row 1/across: 4+5+11+57=77)

MYSTERY SQUARE ANSWER SHEET

4	5	11	**N**
N+1	10	8	1
6	3	**N-1**	12
9	**N+2**	2	7

Lesson 19:
TITHE

 TEACHING GOAL: A tithe, that means one tenth, is a guideline for giving.

1. Play theme song
2. Pray
3. Review last lesson
4. Lesson and discussion
5. Memorize: **Give one; to those who have none.**
6. Close in prayer

 SCRIPTURE: Leviticus 27:30 "A tithe of everything from the land, whether grain from the soil or fruit from the trees, belongs to the LORD; it is holy to the LORD."

Malachi 3:10 "'Bring the whole tithe into the storehouse, that there may be food in my house. Test me in this,' says the LORD Almighty, 'and see if I will not throw open the floodgates of heaven and pour out so much blessing that you will not have room enough for it.'"

 MATERIALS: Groups of ten items: pennies, stuffed animals, dolls, books, cards, fruit, etc. Candy or treat. At least ten items for each child (M&M's) etc.

Words that are written in **bold** are when you, the parent, are speaking. Feel free to use your own words.

Ⓐ Big Idea

Do you know what the word "tithe" means? One tenth or one out of ten items. Have each child count out ten items like pennies, candy, fruit, etc. and then ask them to identify a tenth of each group.

Go to your room and bring back ten of the same kind of item. Suggest collectables or items in which they are currently interested. While they are gathering their own ten items, put away the other groups of ten. **Show me a tenth of what you brought back.**

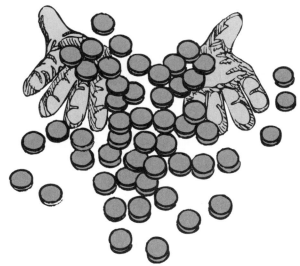

In the Old Testament, God gave us the tithe as a guideline for giving. After the Israelites escaped from Egypt by walking through the Red Sea, they camped near a mountain called Sinai. Moses went up to the top of the mountain to talk with God. God gave him rules and laws for living. The tithe is one of God's rules. Read Leviticus 27:30.

God wants us to give him one tenth of what we have. How can we give God one tenth of what we have? When we give to the church we are giving to God. When we give to others in need we are giving to God. When we give to friends we are giving to God. Talk about how you give to God from the money you make at work.

▶ Activity

Part of growing up and becoming more mature is learning to give. Who thinks they are ready to give? Would you be willing to give a tenth, one of the ten items you have, to someone who doesn't have one? Young kids may have trouble with the idea of giving up something they have. You can reassure them that you are not going to force them to give away their items. Other children may be willing and eager to share what they have.

How did you end up with these ten items? Help them understand that in most cases the items came from others who shared with them or a gift of money from someone else that they used to buy the items. **You have ten because others gave to you. You might want to consider giving one to someone who has none.**

Help your children find a way they can give a tithe of what they have to an organization or friend who can use the item. Allow the reactions and feelings of the children to direct your discussion. Discuss places they can give their items: Give a book to a school so lots of children can read it. Give a book to the church library. Give a toy to a new friend. Give a toy to a missionary to share with children in another country. (Your church may know individuals who are going overseas that might be willing to take the toy.) Give a stuffed animal to a friend who is sick or injured.

I've got a special treat for each of you. Give everyone a piece of candy/gum/treat. **Does that taste good?** Yes. **Would you like more?** Yes! **You can choose to enjoy the one you have or I'll give you ten more if you will give back one of the ten. Who is willing to give me one back if I give you ten more?** Hand out the treats. Count out ten to each and have them give the one back like they promised. Point out that in the same way you gave them treats, God gives us what we have. **In the same way you gave me back one of the treats, God asks us to give back part of what he gives us.**

Application

While they are eating the snack, continue the discussion on tithing. **Was it hard to give me back the one treat?** No, because I had nine others. **This is an important lesson about giving. It is easier to give when we decide in advance to give. It is harder to give something we already have and that we've become attached to.** Discuss how you decide in advance what you are going to give even before you receive a paycheck.

Lesson 20:
HOLY SPIRIT AND THE GLOVE

 TEACHING GOAL: The Holy Spirit in our lives gives our actions meaning.

1. Play theme song
2. Pray
3. Review last lesson
4. Lesson and discussion
5. Memorize: **The Holy Spirit fills us with love; in the same way a hand fits in a glove.**
6. Close in prayer

 SCRIPTURE: Acts 1:8 "But you will receive power when the Holy Spirit comes on you; and you will be my witnesses in Jerusalem, and in all Judea and Samaria, and to the ends of the earth."

Philippians 2:12-13 "Continue to work out your salvation with fear and trembling, for it is God who works in you to will and to act according to his good purpose."

Hebrews 13:20-21 "May the God of peace...equip you with everything good for doing his will, and may he work in us what is pleasing to him, through Jesus Christ."

 MATERIALS: One pair of gloves per team (Form one team to race against the clock or two teams to race against each other)
Watch or timer
One glass of water per team, 3/4 full

Words that are written in **bold** are when you, the parent, are speaking. Feel free to use your own words.

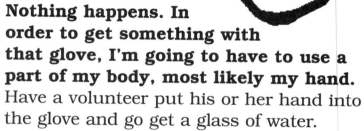

A▶ Big Idea

Lay a glove on the table. **What shape is the glove?** A hand. **I agree. It looks like a hand so it can probably do everything a hand can. "Glove. Get me a glass of water."** Wait for a few seconds.

Nothing happens. In order to get something with that glove, I'm going to have to use a part of my body, most likely my hand. Have a volunteer put his or her hand into the glove and go get a glass of water.

Our life is like the glove and the Holy Spirit is like our hand. It is the Holy Spirit that gives our actions purpose and meaning. We can "do" things all day long, things we think are important, but unless the Holy Spirit is directing us, we will not be accomplishing God's good will and purpose. Read Philippians 2:12 and Hebrews 13:20-21.

B▶ Activity

THE GOAL: Work as a team to transfer the glass of water from person to person using the gloves. If you spill water or touch the glass with anything other than a gloved hand then the team is disqualified from the race.

DIRECTIONS: Each person completes the relay course and transfers the glass of water by following these directions:

- Person #1 puts on the gloves, picks up the glass of water and runs or walks through the relay course.

- Person #1 and Person #2 work together to take off the glove from the free hand and put it on Person #2's hand.

- Pass the glass of water from Person #1's gloved hand to Person #2's gloved hand.

- Person #1 and Person #2 work together to get the second glove onto Person #2's free hand.

- Person #2 runs or walks through the relay course, being careful not to spill any water.

- Repeat until the final person crosses the starting line.

 ## Application

Remember, the hand in the glove represents the Holy Spirit working in our lives. In the same way you needed to have your hand in a glove to complete the relay successfully, we need to have the Holy Spirit in our lives to be successful in accomplishing God's will and good purposes.

Lesson 21:

BOOK OF LIFE
THIS ACTIVITY WORKS BEST WITH THREE OR MORE FAMILIES.

TEACHING GOAL: God keeps a book filled with the name of every Christian. Your name must be in this book to enter heaven.

1. Play theme song
2. Pray
3. Review last lesson
4. Lesson and discussion
5. Memorize: **You'll be heaven bound; when your name in the Book of Life is found.**
6. Close in prayer

SCRIPTURE: Revelation 20:15, 21:27 Your name must be in the Book of Life to get into heaven.

MATERIALS: Phone book
Paper and pen
Tape or stapler

IN ADVANCE: This lesson is best done with another family or two. In advance tell others about your Family Time experience and invite them to join in with you for an evening. Not only will your friends enjoy having Family Time, but they may catch a vision for having their own regular Family Times too.

Words that are written in **bold** are when you, the parent, are speaking. Feel free to use your own words.

 Big Idea

Show the children a local area phone book. **This book contains most of the names of people who live in our**

town or county. Have the children look at how many names there are; then look up neighbors and the families represented at this Family Time.

B Activity

We are going to make our own book of family member names. Take several sheets of paper for each family present, fold them in half, and tape or staple them to look like a book. Make a cover with the words, "The [Your Last Name] Book of Family Names." Write each family member's name in the book. Include members who are not there like grandparents, aunts, uncles, and cousins. **In order to have your name included in the book, you must be a family member. Do we put [a neighbor's name] in this book?** No. **Do we put [a friend's name] in this book?** No.

God has a book in heaven called the Book of Life. Every Christian's name is in that book. A Christian is someone who believes Jesus is the Son of God who came to earth, died on the cross for our sins, and through him we can live with God in heaven for eternity. To get into heaven, you must be a Christian, and your name must be in the Book of Life.

Use a doorway in your home or create a passageway between a piece of furniture and a wall. One adult from each family represented will play the role of the angel Gabriel standing at the opening. Use the family name books created during the activity. Make a single file line in front of the opening. Mix up members from the three families so that family members are not standing next to each other. The first adult playing Gabriel will use their family book and ask each person in line for their name. Gabriel will check their book and only let those whose names are written in their family book pass through. If the person in line is from a different family then their name won't be in the book and they must return to the back of the line. Repeat the activity using a Gabriel from each family so that everyone has an opportunity to go through the gate.

 ## Application

In the same way "Gabriel" only let people through the gate who had their name in the family book, only Christians with their names in the Book of Life will go through the gate to heaven.

This may be an opportunity to ask the question, "Are you in?" Raising the questions in Family Time may be just the preparation needed to later talk individually with your kids to see if they want to trust Christ as Savior.

Index

Seeing is Believing (ALL AGES)

Playing for Keeps (ALL AGES)

Running the Race (ALL AGES)

Wiggles, Giggles, & Popcorn (PRESCHOOLERS)

Index

www.famtime.com

Fun Spiritual Training in Your Home!

For All Ages

For Preschoolers

For Teens

Books in this series by Kirk Weaver

TOOLS FOR FAMILIES

- Free activities
- Activity books for children of all ages—Preschool, Elementary, Junior High, and High School

RESOURCES FOR CHURCHES

- Family Time Team Curriculum
- The Family Time Project: Equipping families through Sunday School, Vacation Bible School, mid-week programs

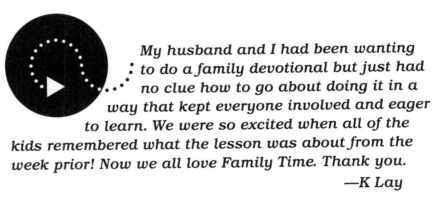

My husband and I had been wanting to do a family devotional but just had no clue how to go about doing it in a way that kept everyone involved and eager to learn. We were so excited when all of the kids remembered what the lesson was about from the week prior! Now we all love Family Time. Thank you.

—K Lay

Family Time Training
5511 S Youngfield St, Littleton, CO 80127
(303) 433-7010 • (866) 433-7010 (toll free)
info@famtime.com

You Will Benefit from
OTHER RESOURCES
for YOUR FAMILY

Discover practical, biblical tools to help you build strong bonds in your relationships at home. Find parenting books, CDs, and DVDs to help you parent from a heart-based perspective. Children's curriculum is available to teach your child the same concepts you are learning. **Free Email Parenting Tips** encourage you on a weekly basis. **Learn more at www.biblicalparenting.org.**

Free
EMAIL PARENTING Tips

Receive practical, biblical parenting advice a couple times a week in your inbox. Sign up online at www.biblicalparenting.org. Also available in Spanish. Visit www.padresefectivos.org.

Sign up for Free Email Parenting Tips now.
(You can remove yourself from the list at any time.) Your email address will not be shared or sold to others.

NATIONAL CENTER *for* BIBLICAL PARENTING

To learn more give us a call or visit www.biblicalparenting.org.

76 Hopatcong Drive, Lawrenceville, NJ 08648-4136
Phone: (800) 771-8334
Email: parent@biblicalparenting.org